ODE TO A TRAFFIC CONE
AND OTHER POEMS

By
Rebecca Goodwin

INVERTED PUBLISHING

i

ISBN: 9780993501647

Table of Contents

TOY STORIES

Rebecca Goodwin

ODE TO A TRAFFIC CONE

Standing there, like a tiny soldier,
How I wish I could just hold ya,
Keeping traffic safe all day,
My only wish, to call you bae,
Nothing else makes me say "Oh damn",
Than when I push you inside my clam.

CONE BUT NOT FORGOTTEN

You tempt me with your bright exterior,
Reflecting all the things I feel,
The way you stand there so superior,
Makes me think this feeling's real.

I know it's wrong but it feels so right,
When I see you keeping traffic safe at night,
It's way too late; it's nearly three,
But this traffic cone is coming home with me!

CHARLES D. SCANLON

Feelings growing,
Goosebumps on my skin
It can't be wrong
when it slides right in,
The hazards tell me
I should be more cautious,
My family's worried,
My dog's getting nauseous

I feel like you may be
My perfect companion,
Though you were invented
By Charles D. Scanlon
But where does the road lead?
The two of us converging,
Is this a dead end
Or just two lanes merging?

ROAD WORKS AHEAD

The best of my partners
was a roadwork abduction
Protecting the cars
From concrete construction
He's mine now,
I love him
He's huge and enormous,
I just wish he could be
More anthropomorphous,

I can't get enough
Of his smooth orange skin
My lips are engorged
And my face starts to grin
When you're in traffic
You're never alone
Everybody needs
Their own traffic cone

It's a journey together,
now he's in my bed,
But I have to be sure
That the road works ahead.

TENTACLE TAKER

Feelings growing
As you push inside
The way it makes me
Want to run and hide
But I mustn't be scared
Of the size and your girth,
Just because you're
The biggest on earth.

Your suckers attract me
And make me feel naughty,
And when I count your inches
And get up to Forty,
I think I've overestimated
The size of my pussy,
I lube up my asshole
And try in my tushy

WONDERFUL TOYS

With toys in hand, I feel incredible
My smile becomes unstoppable
When I want to feel more powerful
My climax is my release
As well as the catalyst
For your knees to become weak

ABOUT A CONE

Do you know what's fun about a cone?
The way they slide
So steadily I can ease over it
angle it around
curve it toward my sweet spot
Incredibly matured
While I go up and down
And listen to all the sounds
From my mouth
and down lower where the fun begins

A NEEDED DISTRACTION

I was so worked up; a head full of noise
My hand migrated to my nearest toys

A cone and a tentacle
you can imagine the rest

Working side by side
I couldn't get any rest

I was too wild and reactive
My hands too utterly distracted

I felt the euphoria so suddenly
I sank deep into my chair
Only to once again feel my fingers
Start to lead my mind elsewhere

IT'S CORN

A farmer's girl
Not a care in the world
A sexual awakening
About to unfurl
Those yellow beads
Really give me the horn,
Drenched in butter so sweet
It's mine
It's corn

I'm tempted and hot
As it's stood on its base,
I'm squatted above it
A smile on my face
I lower myself onto the veg
Within seconds I'm sweating
I'm right on the edge
Of coming so hard
Making perfect porn
Alone in a field with my phone,
It's corn.

WYLD STALLYN

Wanted something different,
Something big and animalistic,
A dildo fit for poetry,
Non verbal, yet linguistic,
A stallion cock would fit the role,
A par for the course,
Cos surely, all my fans
Want to see me fuck a horse.

ONLYFANS BLUES

Rebecca Goodwin

BLACK HOLE BUM

Well, aren't you just a perfect little slut,
Having such a supermassive black hole for a butt,

I can see you've been working on it, don't let me
intrude,
Just looking at that void really puts me in the mood

Just like a black hole in outer space,
Consuming matter, without a trace

An unmissable target, my body flies in,
Never to escape your event whoreizen

Gagging to be filled with cock and cum,
Oh, how I'd love to peg and rim that slutty bum.

These are my thoughts concerning your rectum,
Cos honestly babes, I think it's perfectum.

STUCK WITH YOU

Staring at me when I'm all alone,
You think I don't see you when I'm on my phone,
It falls from my hand and it jams in the sofa,
Now my hand's stuck and you're walking over,
Trying to help with your arms around me,
Hands on my waist, thinking thoughts about me.

Doing my laundry and I know you're there,
Getting so close you can smell my hair,
I bend over like a sitting duck,
But the door slams shut and I'm totally stuck,
You have to help me, come and get a grip,
And then I start to hear your fly unzip!

Renovation time and the house is a mess,
Giant fucking hole in the wall no less,
Think I could fit my whole body inside,
I give it a go but my ass is too wide,
I feel you grab me like I knew you would,
Why does being bad feel so damn good?

Just me and you with your Mum and My Dad,
But I can't help feeling they would be so mad,
If they find out what we do
Because you're my StepBro and I'm stuck with you.

MILKSHAKE

Roses are red, poems are hard
My milkshake brings all the subs to the yard
By the time I'm done, their coals will be charred
Perfect for spitroasting, spice me up and rub it hard

The way you stuff me is a form of art
So tie me up and let the spitroasting start
Baste me with butter but be on guard
The plate will be hot when you serve me a la carte

Devour that juicy thigh, tear those legs apart
Lick that bone and save the lard.

Then have a milkshake
With all the others in my yard.

A HERO IN LEATHER

Leather controls my dominance
Like a whip, it strikes
Pummeling my once lace-driven experiment
I'm owning all
With a more elongated escape
My tongue surrounding
My toys are my cultivated cape

THAT CERTAIN LOOK

There was a certain look

The fire in her hair starting to draw you in

It overtook the rapidly expanding air
While hot breath singed
Your longing and despair

She built mystery within her surroundings
while embers formed

Her limbs tied, her moaning softened
for those who wanted to stare

GOING LIVE

It's a pleasure for you to watch
While hands slide over soft, supple skin
Finding the pleasure that I'm currently in
Vibrations and chills pulse everywhere
Such a warming thrill
Viewing me make subtle noises
When my frenzy is peaking
Finishing vibrations send me there
As I whisper for you to join in too
For far too long you sat;
Merely enjoying the view

EAT ME

Tempting isn't it?
So sugary sweet
My forbidden fruit
Moist enough for you to have as a treat
Wouldn't you like to eat?

THE SKIN THAT I'M IN

A quivering sensation
As my fingers trace my skin
A tingling that travels
Reason to enjoy sin

I'm enjoying the skin that I'm in

I've touched it for so long
But never like this
Now when I feel it
My satisfaction begins

STICKY AND SWEET

Sticky sweetheart,
Rolling in your gleam,
The hand traveling freely
Down the golden seam,
Releasing tensions
And a slight moaning it seems,
When my pearly whites gleam
As my lips live my dreams

DIY

Nothing's more fun than having fun with yourself
All you need are cones, to enjoy everywhere else
Circling inside with well-placed suction
As tightening takes over
My body swelling from seduction

Rapidly wanting more
Before my whole body becomes sore
Too much spanking, you say?
That could never exist
I would love to be spanked all day

I'll do it myself anyway

THAT ONE SUB

Not able to contain it
My lusting uncontrollable
When I catch a glimpse of you
The scenarios you drive my mind to
Watching the screen and hearing the moans
You want to see me join in too, don't you?
Don't worry because I'd already planned to

SAUSAGE INDULGENCE

A juicy sausage, so fresh and grand,
Looking so plump, that I can't stand,
The delicious aroma, calling my name.
I can't wait to indulge in this meaty game.

Succulent and tender, it feels so right,
As my tongue savors each and every bite.
The flavor explodes, like fireworks in the sky,
An experience so fun, I can't help but sigh.

Lost in the moment, I start to suck,
The taste so heavenly, that it's hard to duck.
All the flavors blending in total delight,
I could indulge in it forever, day or night.

So let the juices flow, and the meat unwind,
This sausage indulgence is perfectly designed.
A playful treat, that fills me with joy,
A satisfying pleasure, like a fun toy.

SPUR OF THE MOMENT

The pressure of your pants versus
the pressure of my button both release
A collision of excitement;
a visually entertaining feast
An auditory explosion
When you are expecting it least

PLUG IT IN

Plugging in electricity
From the enticing words I speak,
Your plug fits perfectly
Inside the outlet by my cheek
Come stay a while and get to know me
From the inside out,
Sexual ecstasy I seek

CREAMPIE

Soft and fluffy, like delicate skin,
Sitting on a plate, tempting from within.
Eyes fixated, mouth already salivating,
This is the moment, no more waiting.

Biting through the layers, as the flesh gives way,
The sensation of delight, like sunshine on a gray day.
It's sweet but not overbearing,
Leaving a taste on the tongue, like a rare pairing.

The cream is light, and never too heavy,
It's like sinking in soft flesh, so velvety,
The perfect balance, that sets it apart,
Fulfilling an appetite, that lives in the heart.

As the last morsel surrenders, to its win so divine,
A sense of euphoria, imbues the mind and relaxes
the spine,
It's the joys of a cream pie, that will always remain,
A heavenly indulgence, that's never in vain.

WATCH ME

There are always eyes on you
Those views that build you
They heighten too, from their point of view
Drawing out your inner vixen
While they crave you and your playthings too
Your personality emboldens you
And they want to get to know you

COLLAB

Drink it down,
How sticky sweet the syrup tends to be
You've laid me down,
On top of sheets for all the world to see

You explore me with your tongue
While the handcuffs have won
And I explore with finger nails
To gently scratch you

You shiver with delight
When I grab and start to bite,
Got you wondering what move is next
Anticipation out the window is the best

STEPBROTHER

Getting stuck in places, it's all part of the fun,
To watch my stepbrother rush to see what I've done.
A little bit of mischief, just to play a game,
And let my imagination run absolutely, positively,
insane.

The thrill of adventure, the lure of the scheme,
To make him think that I'm in a terrible dream,
Getting stuck between bars, or inside the washer,
To make him come rescue me, it's so worth the bother.

So let the game begin, and the fun to unfold,
As I find more places, and grow more bold.
But just between you and me, it's all in good fun,
And no one gets hurt, when he fucks my bum.

GIRL/GIRL

Wild inhibitions sparking
Like a candle's flame
Ignited so quickly
Trying to contain
Her groans of pleasure
From being spanked
A pleasurable "pain"
Exploring sexual fantasies
The purpose of the pleasure game

JOIN MY LIVE

Assert confidence and pride
When you want some relief
I'll be right here waiting
A full hour, never brief

Live and ready to chat
Should you choose to have some fun
Just send a little tip
And I'll strip down to my bum

If I've started already
And you missed most of the view
You can happily enjoy the replay
as I've already filmed it for you

TIKTOK

Whether cones are present or not
It could be on steel or counter tops
Washing machines and random spots
Or on a fuck off fancy yacht

Make a Tiktok, choose the sound,
Ideas unbound by my background
Make them laugh and they're always hits
Show some cleavage but not your tits

Angles to try transitions to use
Any thoughts I can amuse
Hands and toys or other parts
Posting a Tiktok is like playing darts
Hit the bullseye or my account departs

INSERTING IDEAS

Blunt is in my nature, and I'm extremely wet
Horny even when my house is a slight mess
Toys laying all around
Photographic equipment
Outfits for posing to reverse your frown
It's all about sometimes laying around
Inserting ideas into me
So you can fantasize about me

CONTROL

Call me daddy, I'm in charge,
Tie my hair back, pull it hard
While you pretend to be in charge
But I control the movement
And you control when you end,
I've already released a few times
While you've stopped yourself, my friend ;)

ACCIDENTAL CREAMPIE

You restrain me, handcuffs firm
My body yearns for your hot sweet sperm
But you don't get to finish yet
The longer we last, the tighter I get
But the tighter I am, the more you enjoy it
And I can feel the throbbing
As you start to deploy it
"Not inside me", I say as you go cross eyed,
"I wanted it all over my glorious backside"
Guess I'll wave that facial cumshot bye-bye,
And resort to a close up of a dripping cream-pie

WINNING IN THE SHOWER

So soft and slippery
Subtle and sweet
My fingers skim through the water
And slide over my sensitive peak
Shower heads create just the right amount of
pressure
First fingertips then fingers find their fun
Filling deep within me until I've won

PRIVATE CHAT

Each inch grows while pleasure rises too
Watching you have fun makes me also want to
Listen to me go wild, watching your exploits
My moans adding to your own never disappoints
Tip again and we'll continue throughout the night
An orchestral explosion of passion and delight

NEW RELEASE

Recording myself dancing
So you don't miss all the things this body can do
Bouncing, sliding down
Lifting my assets up high off the ground
For your pants to rise
Your passions to flare
Your breath to delay
It's my way of giving back to you
So you can re-watch it everyday

PUBLIC

The rush of showing myself in public
Raises my arousal
And the fabric of my shirt
My chest perfectly defined by new bra lines
Freshly washed; newly purchased
Perfectly formed
For us both to admire
As I start to perform

The rush continues as I set up my phone
But footsteps and talking interrupt my groans
The panic of realising I'm no longer alone,
Pull up my panties too late to atone,
They've seen me, they know
Thoughts rushing around
The smile on their face, blushing with fervor
Camera still rolling,
Would you like this to go further?

GODDESS

I need you to obey me
You can only release under my guidance
Keep touching yourself to make me pleased

Do you feel the tension in your jeans?
That's where you go to have a good time
Between your thighs and heavy sighs
Trembling for the fun of it
I rather enjoy witnessing it

GIRL ON GIRL

Are you hot down there?
The fire from my hair is igniting you

While my mouth swirls
My tongue turns

Even higher, my body temperature
makes yours rise too
While I'm in between your thighs
Is that what you'd like for me to do?

PRIVATE SHOW

Care for a private show?
Just whisper to let me know
I'll oblige between my quickening breaths
My throat warmed with anticipation
As you stare at my breasts
This sensation elevating with every second
Your heart's racing
Chasing mine, as I start to beckon,
Finish for me and let me see,
The outcome satisfaction,
For both you and for me

STAR WHORES

In this galaxy so vast and wide,
A place for fun and pleasure welcomes you inside.
Named Star Whores, a strip club in space,
A hub for revelry and hedonistic grace.

Here, space travelers can imbibe and play,
And dancers give performances every day.
Alien races and humans alike,
Enjoy the shows and indulge, taking flight.

With neon lights and music so loud,
The club's atmosphere is nothing but proud.
Lascivious dancers, their moves so sly,
Provide the guests with a feast for the eye.

The party continues all through the night,
With the club's seductive vibe, taking flight.
A place to let go of worries and fears,
And find delight in pleasures that are near.

In the world of Star Whores,
You can leave behind all your chores.
Indulge, dance, but don't use your hands,
You can watch every episode on my OnlyFans.

STEADY RHYTHM

Everyday dreams of lustful reprises
Erotic behavior, meant to keep elevated sizes
Perfecting your technique
to show off lace and lingerie
Hurrying breaths a straining display
Groaning loudly; with climactic praise
A steady rhythm is what truly pays

I JUST WANNA CHILL

"Come on let's work," he said,
Even though I have a sore head
"I don't want to, I need to keep still,
I love you but I just wanna chill"

"But if we don't make videos of your cunt,
How will we eat? It's not like you can hunt"
"Look babe, I'll do it tomorrow I will,
But right now, please I just wanna chill"

"Unprofessional", he says,
Looking down at my gash,
"I only get twenty percent of the cash,
A percentage of nothing is literally nil,
Get off your arse all you do is chill!"

"Fine!" I exclaim and slap on some make up,
Ideas now forming, I'm starting to perk up,
"Let's shoot this and let's shoot that,
Inside and outside, dressed up as a cat
Ten videos shot and ten more would be brill,
You look at me drained, "I just wanna chill!"

BASED ON TRUE EVENTS

Rebecca Goodwin

STEPMUM-AUNTIE

Looking back at when my Dad ran away,
He didn't love me,
As much as my mum's sister's pussay,
He packed his shit and got in her panties,
Now I have mental health issues
And a StepMum Auntie.

My Dad is my Dad and my Uncle too,
Now my cousins are my siblings,
I should really sue,
For the damages, he's caused
Like, I'm real damn cranky,
Cos she's my Step mum
And also my Auntie.

11 INCHES RIPPED MY BUM HOWEL

A collab a little different,
Than what I was used to,
Make up artist and camera man,
Can't believe I chose to
Meet up with Danny again,
This time for anal,
His cock is so big,
I was sure I'd be unable

First in my pussy making me wince,
I take the full measure to the 11th inch,
Then my arsehole is lubed,
Ready for his package,
He's the biggest I've had,
In my back passage

Can't believe my bum is taking that prick,
Packed so full like I'm shitting a brick,

Eruption conclusion,
My bum full of cream,
The video is the most insane you've seen,
Proud of myself for taking eleven inches
Now off to the hospital for several stitches

ADHD IS... Oh look a squirrel

The screen stares back, a blank canvas awaits,
My mind races, ideas tumble, all at a swift rate.
But the doubts of ADHD begin to descend,
My focus falters, and my creativity will suspend.

I need to make content, that's what they want,
Something filthy and fun, not white noise or a taunt.
My fingers fidget, my eyes dart around,
And my thoughts scatter, without a possible rebound.

I look for my notes, which are all over the place,
Ideas scribbled and written, in a scrawling face.
Each note takes me to a different idea, it seems,
Like a million neurons sparking, overriding my
schemes.

The camera rolls, and I start to speak,
But my mind takes a whirl, and all logic leaks.
I ramble and stumble, and lose where I'm headed,
The information I wanted to share now shredded.

It's a constant battle, it's like a merry-go-round,
My mind spinning, never quiet or sound.
The struggle it's real, and it's hard to contain,
Like a wild animal, always hoping to gain.

But I won't let ADHD hold me back,
My content may be scatter-brained, but it's not
off-track.
I accept the quirks and embrace the ride,
Light up a joint and try to unwind.

JOHNNY SINS HAS A SNIFFLE

He's been a teacher, a doctor,
Delivery man, and Preacher
He's been with everyone,
Milfs, Gilfs and twins,
Thought I take a chance
And I messaged Johnny Sins

Asked him to collab
And he said OK,
So I booked a first class ticket,
Headed to LA.

With Dick Bush in tow,
Filming everything,
Spent three days chilling,
Then it was time to do thing thing.

Sat in the bath looking at my phone,
Text message arrived,
He's had to postpone.
But I fly home tomorrow,
Feels like a crime,
This entire trip has been
A waste of my time.

Then a glimmer of hope,
The following morn,
Johnny says he's feeling better
And he's got the horn
No Dick Bush thanks,
He wants to self-shoot,
Fucked for thirty minutes,
Then he came up my chute.

OVERCOME

The scars of childhood, deeply etched,
Abused and wounded, feeling helpless and vexed.
But time has passed, and wounds have healed,
Inner strength and grit, have become my shield.

I refuse to let the past dictate,
Or from my future, take control and manipulate.
I rose above poverty and pain,
Fueled by passion, and a desire to break the chain.

Through hard work and resilience, I overcame,
The struggles of the past, that once caused me shame.
I persevered, despite the odds stacked against,
And moved ahead, with confidence and intensity.

From rags to riches, I have climbed,
Breaking the chains, that once confined.
Happiness and success, now within my grasp,
As I look back, and see how far I have surpassed.

The pain of the past, may never completely fade,
But I have learned to live life, on my own accord
and shade.
A warrior, a survivor, a success story,
A testament to unwavering perseverance, and glory.

SPECIAL KNEES

The morning comes and I start my day,
With the hope to look and feel okay.
But the mirror reveals red, scaly skin,
And I know the day ahead will be tough to begin.

The world expects me to look my best,
But my psoriasis puts me to the test.
The patches on my skin cause me strife,
And I long for freedom from this life.

I try to hide it with clothes and creams,
But the discomfort still invades my dreams.
The stares and whispers hurt me so,
And I feel the need to hide and not show.

But I wish I could embrace my skin,
And feel beautiful and confident within.
To know that I am more than just my flaws,
And stand tall with pride without any pause.

My psoriasis may cause me pain,
But it won't keep me from my gain.
I refuse to let it dampen my spirit,
Or hold me back from owning my merit.

So I take a deep breath and face the day,
With the strength to look past what others might say.
I know that true beauty comes from within,
And my cornflake skin doesn't define everything.

GUYS ARE DICKS

Why, oh why are guys such dicks,
It's like they're braindead
Transfixed on tits
A man with a hard-on,
Is passionate and keen,
And then when he's empty,
He's nowhere to be seen

I'm more than a fuck,
Not just a quick fix,
Why, oh why are guys such dicks.

Then finally you find that one that's distinct,
He's smart and devoted
Could have sworn they're extinct!
But your brain starts to question
His decent exterior
Maybe it's a lie and he has motives ulterior
He's a cheat, a thief, pushing my limits,
And he didn't message back within five minutes

Is it just me?
Is it all in my head?
Wish it was easy for brains to be read,
Dump him, move on,
Not a fan of conflicts,
Why oh why are guys such dicks?

BECKYMIL

Now this is a story all about how
My ass got twisted inside out,
So if you'd like to hear about it
Just sit right there,
I'll tell you all about my arsehole
And what's been in there

From tentacles to traffic cones,
Balls and Blades
Shoving things inside me
Is how I spent most of my days
Filling and drilling
Playing with the grool
And shooting alien eggs inside my hole

When a couple of guys,
Who's credit scores were good,
Started tipping me coin and shaking their wood,
I made a little money and knew what to do,
Became a Millionaire on Onlyfans,
And you can too!

REDHEAD

I dye my hair a bright, bold red,
To stand out from the crowd, that's what I said.
I want to be different, unique, and fun,
And feel like I'm the only one.

With every stroke of the brush and dye,
I imagine the stares, the looks, the why.
My hair, a bold statement for all to see,
A reflection of my individuality.

I love the fiery hue and its sparkle so wild,
And just for a moment, I feel beguiled.
But deep down, I know this moment will pass,
And I'll have to go back to my old, bland mass.

When the time comes for the dye to fade,
I'll go back to the blonde, a color with grace.
And with every strand, I'll hope to blend in,
No recognition of the person that's within.

Maybe then, I'll be free from society's eyes,
That judge unfairly, only to chastise.
But until that day, I'll enjoy being red,
And stand proud with color on my head.

EVERYONE IN PORN IS ON THE SPECTRUM

Everyone in porn is on the spectrum,
A vast and varied range,
From the perversions of introversion,
To the heights of extroverted change.

Some navigate porn quite comfortably,
In collabs or one-on-one,
While others find themselves more at ease,
Shoving traffic cones up their bum.

Some brains are wired quite differently,
They delve into detail, and fixate,
While others see the bigger picture,
And create, and innovate.

Some feel, tweet, and share online,
In words that pour out endlessly,
While others scroll in silence,
Containing what they feel, tenaciously.

But the spectrum is not a line,
Nor is it just black and white,
It's full of varying delicious colours,
And it's a beautiful sight.

For though we may seem different,
And at times may feel deflated,
We must remember that together,
Is how content gets created.

SEXTING

I'm a content creator, it's my claim to fame
I sext all day long, and it's never mundane
I get so creative, it's almost obscene
My words can be naughty, and a bit too keen

I chat about sucking and sometimes lust
It's not always easy, but it's a must
I can be tongue-in-cheek, or straight to the point
Sometimes I'm subtle when I've had a joint

Sexting is never dull, always with a twist
I want your dick, and sometimes a fist
I'm living my dream, just writing away
And if people like it, then it's a great pay day.

THE SHOWERHEAD

As the water cascades and streams,
She stands beneath the shower head, it seems,
A woman enthralled in the moment,
Her enjoyment of such simple pleasure quite potent.

The water's heat, melting away the day,
Relaxing, soothing, in every way,
She closes her eyes, and takes deep breaths,
Feeling the water beat down like a lover's caress.

The shower head, her trusted ally,
A companion through times good and wry,
As its streams of water wash away,
The tears and fears of yesterday.

In this sacred place, she stands tall,
Free to be herself, to let it all fall,
The shower head, her secret keeper,
Sharing in her moments of personal leisure.

Alone with her thoughts, and the sound of water,
The world outside, doesn't really matter,
For in this moment, she knows what's true,
Simple joys like these can be a source of renewal.

MONEY MATTERS

Money matters, they say with a grin,
But when you're a millionaire, it's a constant din.
Everyone wants a piece of the pie,
But little do they know, it's harder to satisfy.

Friends come calling with a smile,
But their intentions are anything but guile.
They offer drinks and meals galore,
But money can't buy true happiness, that's for sure.

Family members see dollar signs,
And think they should get their fair share in kind.
But they forget the hard work and the strife,
That led to the fortune amassed in life.

So being a millionaire is a double-edged sword,
As everyone around starts to horde.
But one thing is certain, this I'll decree,
True wealth is measured in more than just currency.

AIM FOR THE HOWEL

When language is your only tool,
And your accent makes people drool,
Pronouncing words can be a feat,
Especially for visitors you'll meet.

And if by chance, your tongue does stray,
And transforms "hole" in a curious way,
Do not despair, do not mourn,
For a lifeless language is one to scorn.

Instead, embrace the art of speech,
And the way different pronunciations can reach.
For "Howel" may sound silly and queer,
But to some, it might inspire a cheerful cheer.

Language is not just about being precise,
It's about expression, to be yourself, and that's nice.
So embrace your accent, and don't let it throttle,
For it's part of you, and it's what makes you special.

ETHOT BLUES

A Tiktok creator, with charm and grace,
Teasing the guys, all over the place,
Putting on a show, to get those views,
But it's getting old, and it's time to choose.

Is it worth it, to fake and create,
When it's not the real me, but only bait,
To get those followers and likes galore,
But a facade of happiness I can't adore.

Putting up a front, day after day,
Makes me feel like a puppet on display,
Though it may seem like tons of fun,
In truth, it's just work undone.

The burden of playacting, is getting too much,
I long for honesty, and being truthful as such,
Not having to pretend, that I'm someone else,
For authenticity, is key to finding oneself.

So the tease and the flirts will soon be no more,
For the real me, is worth fighting for,
I'd rather be angry, than a fake façade,
For truth and authenticity, are traits to applaud.

A WINNING SMILE

A smile that once caused me so much grief,
Crooked and stained, it was beyond relief,
But now, I have a grin that's proud and true,
All thanks to new crowns, shining bright and new.

The process was long, but oh so worth it,
To have a smile that feels like such a perfect fit,
Gleaming and white, like a sunny day,
A facelift that has given me a whole new way.

I can't help but smile, with a newfound pride,
For years, I had to hide behind my lips, so shy,
But now, my teeth are like an artist's canvas,
Making me feel more confident, just fabulous.

So here's to Dental Design, and the smile they bring,
A new beginning, after years of hiding,
For a smile is more precious than riches or gold,
A symbol of joy, and a story yet untold.

ENDGAME

Years of hustle in front of the screen,
Creating content that still leaves us keen,
But it's time to slow down and take a deep breath,
The endgame is here, it's time for the next step.

Retiring from the spotlight and stepping down,
From being an onlyfans creator, wearing the crown,
It's time to get serious, and invest in the new,
The world of real estate, and success to pursue.

The dream of owning property by the
cosmopolitan sea,
Is now within reach, as I can travel with glee,
No more late-night editing or endless promotion,
Retiring from onlyfans fame, a notion we always
wanted.

The hustle doesn't stop, it just changes direction,
A new beginning, a fresh perception,
Investing the time and effort into the "what's next",
The endgame is just the beginning, and we're
ready for success

BeckyMil.com

Printed in Great Britain
by Amazon

22588934R00047